Pinterest
Ultimate Guide

How to use Pinterest for Business and Social Media Marketing

Lance MacNeil

Table of Contents

Introduction

One of the hottest social networking sites today is Pinterest. Although the site still lags behind global behemoths Facebook and Twitter in terms of number of registered users, Pinterest has nonetheless had a steady and progressive rise over the years, thanks in large part to its heavy focus on gorgeous images. The site's enormous success is definitely one for the books. Latest figures show that Pinterest has over 70 million registered users across the world, with a huge bulk of them - or more than 50 million users - coming from the United States alone.

According to webpage ranking service, Alexa, Pinterest is the 27th most frequently visited website in the world. Without a doubt, Pinterest definitely counts as a total force to reckon with in the social media sphere. That's a giant leap from its initial days in 2010, the year it was founded by Paul Sciarra, Evan Sharp, and Ben Silbermann.

With over 300 people currently employed by Pinterest, it continues to forge ahead as it battles it out for social media supremacy against both new and established competitors.

Chapter 1: What is Pinterest?

Pinterest is an online visual bulletin board. It is a relatively new social sharing website that is sweeping the nation. You choose an image that you like and pin it on a board that you name. From fitness to food, to photography and art, there are unlimited possibilities with Pinterest. What seems like a simple concept is simply addictive.

Think of this website as visual image of everything beautiful. People pin things to a virtual pin-board. All the things that you would traditionally cut out from a magazine or print off the internet are no longer necessary. The days of cutting pictures from a magazine, articles, and recipes are long gone. You can pin any image to a board on your Pinterest account. You can follow other people's boards, you can follow friend's boards, friends can follow you, it's a lot like facebook and twitter in that respect to sharing and amplification of what you are posting.

Pinterest is used by and large as a visual discovery tool. It's a bookmarking site that is both social and visual, which means users can share their media content (known as pins) to other users. These pins are generated on an average of two million each day. The images are either sourced from the world wide web or uploaded by the users themselves.

They can later be organized according to themes in collections known as pin-boards.

Predominantly female users

One of the remarkable things about Pinterest is that it has a predominantly female population. More than 80 percent of registered and active users of the social media site are women who come from different age brackets, income ranges, and nationalities. In fact, 92 percent of all pins and 94 percent of all activities on the site are made by women.

Because of the disproportionate number of female users, much of the content seen on the site caters to themes or subjects that are traditionally associated with women, including fashion, baking, interior design, inspirational quotes, and weddings. This is precisely the reason why Pinterest has, on certain occasions, been referred to as a "pink ghetto," or a domain exclusively run by women. Another remarkable thing about Pinterest is its immense effectivity as a marketing tool. Pinterest, for instance, has a much higher conversion rate as opposed to Twitter or Facebook. This means your content is likelier to generate more views and shares (and possibly higher sales returns) if it were posted on Pinterest than anywhere else. The high conversion rate is attributed to the visual nature of the site; users are more likely to click on a beautiful image rather than read about it in a block of text.

Data from the Pew Research Center's Internet & American Life Project also shows that many of Pinterest's users belong to the upper middle and upper segments of the income stratum, with about 20 percent of total users coming from homes with a total household income that exceeds $75,000. This explains the higher spending of Pinterest users on products recommended on the site than the spending of users on other sites.

For people or organizations wanting to make the transition to Pinterest, there are no hard and fast rules that will guarantee your success on the site. As with other social networking sites, much of how you will fare on Pinterest will be dependent on the way you execute your marketing goals and objectives.

In general, there are a number of things you can subscribe to in order to ensure that you maximize the full potential of Pinterest in helping you see positive results. First thing you need to remember, you need quality content.

Emphasis on quality images

Pinterest users will tell you that image is everything. Given its visual nature and heavy focus on compelling and beautiful content, whether or not you will thrive on this site will largely be determined by the quality of the images you pin. Blurry, poorly lit, and low-resolution images are an exception than the rule on Pinterest, and pinning any image of this sort is bound to yield unflattering feedback from other users. If you are cautious of how your brand is seen or viewed, the last thing you want to commit is pin a crappy photo.

One of the nice features of Pinterest is the ability to create pin-boards. Here, you organize your content based on a specific theme so that other users will not have to swim through random content. In making pin-boards, you have to be very strategic. Consider your target audience first: Who are they? What do they want? How can you make them look at your content?

Just as importantly, you need to pin regularly. The more you pin and re-pin images, the easier it will be for you to carve your niche on the site. Beware, however, from flooding the site by pinning content one after the other. You want to space out each pin evenly so that you don't end up annoying your followers with your relentless pinning.

At the same time, make sure to include snappy, SEO-ready captions to each media you pin, preferably with hashtags at the end. This will make it easier for users to find your content when they search using relevant keywords on the site's built-in search engine.

The same is true with the About Page. Each account on Pinterest comes with a section where you can introduce yourself or your organization. Make use of this section to advertise what your business is all about. Try to make this section brief by focusing on relevant keywords only. There is no need at all to write your company history in here.

Establishing relationships

Most importantly, do not forget the social aspect of Pinterest. Your account should not be on Pinterest just for the sake of being there. This site works best when you engage with your followers and other users.

Begin by following relevant users. Check out similar businesses on the site and look at who they are following. A good rule of thumb is to follow the so-called influencers or users with the most number of followers, and build a relationship with them. This can be done by re-pinning their content or leaving comments on their boards.

At the same time, do not forget the users who leave comments on your pins. Make it a point to reply to them if you can. The key is to build trust and loyalty with your intended demographic. Once you have captured your desired market, it's going to be a lot easier to frame your subsequent pins.

Outside of Pinterest, make sure your website or blog has the corresponding Pinterest "Pin It" button. This is to make it easier for your readers to pin your content without having to copy and paste the URL of your site.

As a social networking site, Pinterest definitely shows a lot of promise, particularly in its use as a visual discovery mechanism. It is also a great addition to your arsenal of marketing tools, especially since it has been proven to work wonders for thousands of brands that now find it indispensable.

Chapter 2: Is Pinterest the New Social Media King?

There was a fair amount of skepticism when social media site Pinterest was launched in 2010 by American technopreneurs. In a highly competitive field dominated by two global giants, Facebook and Twitter, many pundits wondered whether a previously unheard of start-up can manage to carve its own niche.

Four years later, Pinterest managed to survive the tough competition. Now the third leading social media site on this part of the universe, right behind Facebook and Twitter, Pinterest has proven its resilience by underscoring its own unique benefits and focusing on a visually appealing approach rather than posing as a poor imitation of other popular sites.

Without a doubt, Pinterest definitely counts as a total force to reckon with in the social media sphere. Given its enormous success over the years, is Pinterest now the new social media king?

Influence on trends and consumer choices

The power and influence of Pinterest in shaping media trends and consumer choices is inarguable, but to allude to it as the new social media king may be a little inaccurate, or premature. But the consistently dismal number of male users on Pinterest does not seem to cause any serious dent on the social media site's overall performance. If anything, this even works to its advantage.

Consider the diversity of women on the site: Data from the Pew Research Center's Internet & American Life Project shows that as of February 2013, Pinterest is populated by well-to-do users, with about 20 percent of users having a total household income that exceeds $75,000, while only 10 percent of its users have a total household income under $30,000.

In addition, a more recent study by Forrester early this year revealed that majority of Pinterest users belong to Generations Z and Y, with each generation accounting to 27 percent of total users respectively. These are followed by members of Generation X running not too far behind at 19 percent, Baby Boomers at 14 percent, while members of the Golden Generation constitute the minority at six percent. The mix of users on Pinterest allows it to become the social media site with the highest conversion rate, far exceeding those by Facebook and Twitter. Companies and organizations that tap Pinterest as part of their marketing strategies have shown positive results as a result of traffic generated by their content pinned on the site.

Compelling images

One of the reasons for Pinterest's success is its heavy focus on compelling and beautiful images. Even a cursory look at the millions of pins that comprise the site would yield the inevitable conclusion that much of its drawing power rests on the mosaic of gorgeous images pinned by many users across the globe.

And since much of the content on Pinterest is curated by women for women, the social media site has become the de facto go-to destination for people looking to see novel ideas and the latest trends in the field of culinary arts, fashion, design, and weddings, among many others.

In fact, 2012 data from Repinly, a data directory service that collates numbers and figures from Pinterest, says 29.5 percent of the most popular pins on the site belong to the food and drinks category, followed by the arts and crafts category at 13.4 percent.

The heavy focus on images caters to the popular notion of the Internet as an inherently visual medium, driven in large part by the visual culture espoused by many netizens. In addition to photos, users of the site can also pin videos and infographics from all corners of the Internet.

Another thing that makes Pinterest a necessary marketing tool for people and businesses is the fact that its users are also spenders. In other words, these users do not simply browse or merely pin content themselves, they also have a stronger tendency to shell out cash for items that fancy them. In fact, data shows that almost half of US web-based consumers made a purchase based on Pinterest recommendations.

Impact on consumer spending

This is in stark contrast to data from Facebook and Twitter. While the two are useful in site referrals and information dissemination, the two do not have the same effect Pinterest has in terms of consumer spending.

This harks back to the visual nature of Pinterest, where users (and potential customers) get to have a good luck at the products that are offered. As a consequence, it is not as hard to convince them to purchase something, especially when the product on hand presents itself as a good buy.

The compelling image essentially does all the talking, and when this same image is re-pinned multiple times, the impact it could have on sales is going to be very significant.

These data and figures underscore the important role Pinterest plays for people or organizations wanting to maximize their marketing options. In the past, many marketers relied solely on Facebook and Twitter to spread the word out on their products and services, improve brand recognition, increase audience engagement, and boost sales.

Many were skeptical about adding another social media account in their arsenal of marketing tools, especially since managing multiple accounts requires efficiency, strategic timing, and constant production of content.

These days, however, businesses are trooping to Pinterest en masse, especially in light of the largely positive data yielded by those who took the time and initiative to set up their own accounts. Higher conversion rates on Pinterest means that for many businesses, their content gets to attract much higher views, likes, and shares. More importantly, increased customer engagement along with more positive brand reputation results in better returns. What's not to like with this set-up?

The past four years have shown what this crafty, visually appealing social media site is capable of; it is no small feat that it has managed to rise from a relatively obscure site to the world's leading destination for visual inspiration. In the end,

Pinterest may not exactly be the new social media king, but it is certainly the queen.

Chapter 3: The Basics of Marketing in Pinterest

Pinterest is currently one of the most popular websites on the internet. This website is intended to help people create a database of links, images and videos of things that matter to them.

Though it is mostly dubbed as a crafter and DIY lovers' website, more and more people are joining Pinterest and reaping the benefits of creating and sharing a series of boards (collections of an idea) for inspiration, planning and organizing events or saving links, images, and videos on an online platform.

This free website is founded on the idea of a "personalized social media platform" that people can use and share for specific purposes. It allows people to save a link, image or video by "Pinning" it on a "Board". The board serves as an organizing tool, like a category for different topics that hold "Pins" that fall under the category.

Pinterest holds a large demography of users ranging from teenagers to adults, most of which are women. It is often compared to Google because it not only allows people to store pins and boards, but for research and discovering new websites and new ideas on the internet.

Bloggers, photographers, writer, illustrators and known personalities have been using Pinterest to share their interest and visual inspiration to their audience. Aside from its popularity, it also hosts different opportunities and advantages for businesses.

Because of this, it continues to attract businesses to open Pinterest accounts and use it to tap their audience and attract more visitors to their websites. Pinterest is connected to different social media platforms including Twitter, Facebook and YouTube.

Users can automatically share their pins with just a click to all these social media sites, allowing their followers to view the pins even without a Pinterest account. The website also makes it easier for companies to create an online catalogue of products and items. Pinterest users and customers find it easier to shop, by simply browsing through the companies' boards and clicking on the image that directs them to the actual webpage. It also gives the company an opportunity to be discovered by Pinterest users by using tags and categories.

There are basic steps and strategies to use Pinterest in improving and curving the growth of a business upward. Here's a guideline of basic steps that websites can do to improve their business:

1. *Profiling*

After creating a Pinterest account, make sure to feature the name of the business and include a link of the website. Add an interesting but informative paragraph about the business. This will be shown in the "About" section and will appear below the profile photo of the account. A good and interesting profile will help gain followers and entice other Pinterest users to check out the profile.

2. *Connect to Social Media Sites*

Connect the Pinterest account to various social networking sites including Facebook, Twitter and YouTube. Also add a "Pin" button to the website to help direct visitors to the Pinterest account. If the business has a blog, put up the Pinterest account on the blog.

3. *Start Pinning*

Create boards with creative and interesting names. Use this feature to pin products and images from the website. Add a caption and input tags. Use popular but related keywords to help other pinners discover the image posted on the Pinterest profile.

4. *Connect with other Pinterest Users*

Follow other Pinterest users. Comment on different pins and follow their board. It's also a good idea to join a "shared board". A shared board allows various Pinterest users to add their own Pins to the board as long as it fits the category of the board. This will help other people discover the pins of the website or business. It's also a great opportunity to start connecting with people and build a network of connections, people to collaborate with in the future.

5. *Variety*

Though it is important to showcase the products and images of the website, it is also important that the boards contain a variety of Pins from different websites. Pin interesting and captivating photos from different websites. Never pin an image directly found on Google Images. It is best to pin it from its original source. Consider pinning videos. Pinning videos is not very popular in Pinterest. If one wants to separate themselves from other pinners, try doing this.

6. *Share on SNS*

Aside from connecting the Pinterest account to social media accounts, use these SNS accounts to share the Pins on the Pinterest account. This will help increase traffic and followers.

7. *Optimize*

Optimize the website to automatically include a Pin button for each post and image. This will make it easier for other Pinterest users to share the image or link on their own profiles.

8. Watermark

Add a watermark or logo to the original images used in the website. This will ensure that no one takes credit for the images when it is shared and pinned in various Pinterest accounts. However, when creating a watermark, make sure it doesn't block the entire photo. Position it in a way where it won't distract viewers.

9. RSS Feed

Every Pinterest account has its own RSS feed. You can use the RSS feed to advertise on various social networking sites so visitors can follow and be updated with new posts and pins.

Pinterest is a very effective marketing strategy when done properly. Take this opportunity to increase the audience and visitors of the website. Also, use this opportunity to start connecting with popular Pinterest users, including bloggers. Propose partnership or collaboration plans. This will help increase the customers of the business and increase the traffic on your website.

Aside from that, Pinterest makes it easier for other people to include the images and videos on the website in their own visual boards that they share with other people. It is also an engaging and creative way of cataloguing products and featuring campaigns and other advertisements.

The internet has changed the way business marketing is conducted. It has opened many new opportunities and possibilities to reach people from all over the world. It has provided a platform for customers from different countries to browse through websites and purchase from companies and businesses online.

Pinterest is just one of the platforms that has revolutionized and continues to redefine how marketing and advertising is done. Not only is it a friendly website and application, it also provides a cost-less avenue to market products, promote campaigns and advertisements; giving young businesses an opportunity to thrive and grow.

It has even surpassed other networking sites in terms of traffic and influence including LinkedIn, StumbleUpon and YouTube. While there are people who are busy using Pinterest for social and personal reasons, others are using it to connect and engage with customers in a visual, creative and appealing way.

Look into the possibilities of using Pinterest in business plans and campaigns and see how it affects the growth of a business or website.

Chapter 4: Advance Marketing Skills in Pinterest

Since Pinterest was introduced to the public, thousands of people have been enamored and drawn to using it. Pinterest is an online database intended to store, organize and share ideas, collections and inspiration in a creative and visually appealing way.

Though Pinterest is popularly known as a crafter's website filled with DIY images, articles and videos, it doesn't confine itself to these topics alone. Millions of Pinterest users are pinning and creating boards about various topics including designs, multimedia, photography, home improvement, health, fashion, fitness and architecture. It basically stores any information that a pinner wants to share and save in his or her boards.

But while thousands of pinners are focused on using Pinterest for personal purposes, others are monetizing and using it for business and marketing purposes. Bloggers, websites and online shops are using it to promote their products and encourage pinners to visit their website and browse through their pins and boards.

Even though one has learned the basics of marketing and advertising in Pinterest, there's always room for improvement. There are several ways to further widen and strengthen the influence and effect of a Pinterest account to customers and internet users. Here are some tips for advanced marketing and advertising in Pinterest.

1. Tagging

This recently added feature allows Pinterest users to tag others in their pins. When used correctly, it can increase the number of followers and attract more visitors, especially when the tagged person in the pin is popular and has a lot of followers in Pinterest. Try tagging the original source of pin when re-pinning it in a board. It is also an effective way of connecting or starting a business relationship with another pinner.

2. Catalogue

Use Pinterest to create an online catalogue of products and services. Include a description of the product or service. Make it enticing and informative as much as possible. When doing this, always include the price of the product. It makes it easier for pinners to purchase a certain product in Pinterest when there's enough information about the product.

3. Campaign

Depending on the type of business, use Pinterest to create campaigns and interesting boards. For instance, if the business is an online fashion store, include a board for a spring, summer, fall, and winter collection. Create a board with styling and fashion tips. This will catch the attention of pinners. Remember, interesting and informative pin will encourage a pinner to follow other accounts and profiles.

4. *Alternative Description and Image Filename*

When uploading a photo on a website that will be used for pinning, avoid using a generic filename like IMG568. A filename like this limits the chances of people seeing it on the internet. Instead, learn to add alternative descriptions and filenames.

Make the filenames as specific as possible. For instance, a picture of a shoe product should have a filename containing basic information about the shoe like its color and style. When pinning the image, include a description of the product and use popular tags and keywords.

5. *Be verified*

Like Facebook, Twitter and YouTube, Pinterest now offers the   verification feature. What does it do? The verification simply verifies and informs users that a certain Pinterest account is real. A verified account helps in gaining followers since it shows that the account is real and not a scam. This also prevents other people from pretending to be another person. A verified account also enables Pinterest user to access Pinterest Analytics.

6. *Pinterest Analytics*

Pinterest Analytics is similar to Google Analytics. It helps users to monitor the progress of their profiles, find the source of traffic, find out which pin gathers the most visitors, and response to which keyword is the most searched and used in the site. You can use this method to improve the statistics of a Pinterest page. If a certain keyword draws more customers than others, use it more often. Monitor the trends and pattern pins, boards and keywords according to the trends.

7. *Engage*

Connect with pinners. Respond to comments and write descriptions as engaging as possible. Avoid simply writing informative descriptions. Write each description with an engaging sentence or question that will encourage pinners to comment and voice their opinions.

This will also help in monitoring which products get the most response or determine how satisfied customers are when it comes to products and services offered by a business or company.

8. Testimonials

Create a board solely for testimonials and reviews of products and services. When doing this, make it as interesting and creative as possible. It can be a video clip of several customers reviewing the product or giving testimonials or a photo of the customer with a snippet of the review that links to an article or blog post.

9. Coupons and Behind the Scenes

Use Pinterest to post and share coupons or special promos. Create visually appealing and interesting coupons that pinners can appreciate as an art or inspiration. Also add a behind the scenes board for photo shoots, campaigns, events or making the products. This will help pinners and customers visualize how the products are made or how an event was organized.

10. Contests

Contests and giveaways are effective in increasing followers and web traffic. Post giveaway or contest details on Pinterest and include it in the rules and guidelines. It can even be used to promote products and services from the website by asking readers and pinners to create a board about the products they want to have or products that inspire them. Their

Pinterest followers and friends will most likely participate in the contest and those are additional visitors, followers or customers to a website.

There are many ways to use Pinterest. One of the most advantageous ways is to use the Pinterest market to promote products and campaigns. Though using Pinterest for marketing purpose seems like a lot of work it's definitely worth the effort.

Marketing in Pinterest doesn't have to be too serious; you can just enjoy pinning or engage with other users. Remember, hard work pays off at the end.

Pinterest also improves the creativity and marketing skills of a person. It's a great avenue to display design skills and to come up with a unique ways to present ideas, inspirations and products to pinners, readers and customers. Use it to learn from other businesses and discover new ways to promote and advertise products and services.

Advanced marketing in Pinterest doesn't necessarily mean advanced skills in using the internet. In fact, it doesn't even involve using or making HTML codes. Instead, it's about learning to turn situations into an advantage that will help a business grow and thrive. It's all about creativity, people skills and of course, business and marketing skills.

Pinterest does not limit a person's capabilities, rather improves it and widens the horizon of possibilities. Use this opportunity to take a business to a new level and reach new milestones and goals.

Chapter 5: Attracting more followers on Pinterest

With over 70 million users and counting, Pinterest is fast emerging as one of the hottest social media networking sites today. Its focus on beautiful and compelling images makes it a standout from other equally popular sites. In fact, it now even serves as the go-to destination for online users wanting to learn more about wedding preparations, pick up new baking recipes, learn about exciting travel destinations, and in general cultivate a sense of visual inspiration.

There are a number of advantages and benefits on why creating a niche on Pinterest makes for a smart marketing strategy as far as you or your organization is concerned.

For starters, there's money to be made on Pinterest. Unlike Facebook or Twitter where the most you can do is create hype for your brand, on Pinterest you can reasonably expect to generate leads and actual sales. Did you know, for example, that half of those who have seen product recommendations on Pinterest eventually end up availing them?

One of the biggest mistakes many new Pinterest users commit, however, is the tendency to focus heavily on acquiring followers without first checking their own content. Whether you like it or not, the quality of your pins will by and large determine either the success or failure of your managed account.

Pinterest allows you to create comprehensive visual bookmarks of webpages that can be shared socially. Emphasis should be duly placed on the word "visual." In a site with millions of gorgeous images, the key challenge lies in how to make your original content stand out.

Content is king

The answer is fairly simple: create quality content. Do not pin blurry, out of focus, pixelated, poorly lit, or overly saturated photos. Strive to produce images that tell a story or convey a sense of drama.

On average, a pin on Pinterest gets re-pinned at least 10 times. So in general, the sharper and prettier the image, the better chances of being shared and creating a buzz to your account. But pinning gorgeous images on your account is not enough. More importantly, you have to write effective and concise captions that are specific and SEO-rich.

You can also write hashtags at the end of your captions. Remember, an integral aspect of increasing the number of your followers is having an easy accessibility of your content. You can't have followers if you have obscure and hard to find pins.

At the same time, be mindful of the frequency with your content. Try to update your pin-boards on a regular basis, but make sure to even out the intervals between each post. After all, you do not want to flood others with your content.

Note that pinning regularly makes your account exciting and provides your followers something to look forward to. If you do not pin on a regular basis, you miss out on two things:

First, other Pinterest users will be turned off by your inactivity. Second, you would lose out on the opportunities for leads and sales that could have otherwise been generated by new and updated pins.

A very crucial aspect of getting more followers is placing a heavy emphasis on the social nature of Pinterest. So check out accounts similar to yours and follow them. Find out the most popular users and engage with them either by leaving comments on their pins or mentioning them on your posts.

Enhanced social engagement

Acknowledge the other users who follow you or take time to leave comments on your account. Try to respond to their comments if you can in order to build greater social engagement within your pin boards.

In creating these pin-boards, you should always know your audience. You should know their wants, needs, and their preferences so it will be much easier to create a customized experience for them.

The more dynamic your account, the better it is. To help you identify the kind of pins that will generate the most buzz or interest, have a social media calendar ready. Identify the holidays, occasions, or events that call for specific posts.

Christmas, Valentine's Day, Mothers' and Fathers' Days, end of school, the start of spring break, Fourth of July, Thanksgiving Day, and other momentous days signify an opportunity to get in touch with certain audiences. This targeted approach in pinning content will certainly maximize the exposure of your account and increase the chances of attracting new followers.

A sure way to create buzz, however, is by sponsoring contests and promotions. Guaranteeing exciting prizes always makes for a good marketing strategy as long as your contests are entertaining and easy to participate in. Require all contestants to follow your account. For instance, offering a chance to win a prizes is an easy and relatively hassle-free way of collecting more followers to your account. Just be sure to follow through with the promise to avoid negative backlash.

Optimizing your own webpage

Outside of Pinterest, there are also a handful of things you can do to make others be familiar with your account and become eventual followers themselves. One of the things you can do is insert the Pinterest button on your website or blog. Place this button at the end of each article or right next to an image on your webpage to make it easier for your web visitors to re-pin your content.

You can also create a Pinterest widget and place it on a prominent part of your page. This widget is supposed to show a glimpse of your pins and pin boards in order to entice others to go check your account.

And finally, do not forget to link your Pinterest account with your other social media networks. This is to make managing your accounts more efficient, seamless, and integrative. Link your Pinterest account, for example, with Facebook or Twitter to let others know your new pins.

At the same time, you can also try to pin the images on your Instagram or Facebook account, or create special pin boards based on the content from your other social media feeds. The possibilities are endless. You just need to be imaginative, creative, and strategic.

In sum, Pinterest serves as a great marketing tool for people or organizations that want to boost their company profile, enhance traffic to their content, or improve their bottom line.

Take note, however, that similar to the case of Facebook and Twitter, having more followers isn't necessarily better, especially when a huge bulk of your followers do not have a stake in your organization's overall goals and objectives. So in trying to increase your followers on your Pinterest account, it is important that you end up attracting the kind of crowd that you want, the kind that will promote greater customer engagement and enhance the performance of the products or services you offer.

You can do this by being strategic and by spending a fair amount of time producing quality content, interacting with your followers, and optimizing your own blog or website. The strategies listed above should serve as effective measures to kick start your journey to eventual success on Pinterest.

Chapter 6: Pinterest for Business and Marketing

It is common for people to use the Internet to search for all kinds of information. While a diverse amount of data can be found in an instant, keeping all those searched information organized and accessible can often be difficult and overwhelming.

Pinterest is now considered an important aspect of most B2B or B2C social media marketing strategies. It is practically a database of things that people would like to have or find interesting, which may be a valuable piece of information to marketers and advertisers.

While Google analyzes numbers to figure out what is significant, Pinterest users already define and emphasize what is relevant for a given topic.

As the third most popular social networking website in the world, Pinterest can be a great tool for ecommerce stores to increase their website traffic and boost sales and finance. From the traffic generated by Pinterest, shoppers are 10 percent more likely to make a purchase compared to those who arrive from other social sites.

According to data, 43 percent of Pinterest users interact with retailers or businesses they like on the site, compared with 24 percent of Facebook users.

Seventy percent of the surveyed users said they use Pinterest to get ideas on what to purchase. Consequently, Pinterest is now perceived to be a very popular driver of in-store sales.

In fact, over twenty percent of the Pinterest users that were surveyed said they bought an item from the actual store after pinning, re-pinning, or liking it.

To best optimize Pinterest for businesses, here are some suggestions:
Complete and enhance your company or business profile. Make sure that the Pinterest profile features the following:

- A significant image that represents your business and preferably one that matches your other social networks (Twitter, Facebook Page, etc.) for easier recognition by your target audience.

- Include a short profile of the business that briefly explains your identity and encourage people to learn more about you. This should be consistent as well with your profile on your other social networks or website.

- Include your verified website so that your Pinterest profile visitors can instantly refer or be linked to your official website.

- Include a clickable link to your Twitter and Facebook accounts as well.

Create boards on your Pinterest account that relate to keywords for which you would like to rank on google. For example, a caterer may want to create boards for wedding parties, family reunions, events and other types of services. Apart from the SEO factor, your visitors can get a quick insight into what your business is about and what you have to offer.

Pin images and videos based on your target audience's interests and behavior. In content marketing, the goal is to create content that your target audience and potential customers will be drawn to.

Monitor the pinning activity from your website. Just like how you acknowledge the people who re-tweet you on twitter or share content from your Facebook Page, you may also want to interact with those who have pinned images directly from your website.

Conclusion

Given the right social media strategy and implementation, Pinterest may actually offer any business more referral traffic than twitter, and perhaps generate more leads than LinkedIn, Google + and YouTube combined.

It may even have the power to convert more fans into paying customers who will easily share your content with their friends.

In just a few years after it was launched, Pinterest surpassed ten million users, faster than any other stand-alone site in history. It now has the potential to drive a significant amount of referral traffic to your website, and at the same time boost actual sales. That idea perhaps is valid enough for any business to consider using Pinterest.

Made in the USA
Middletown, DE
16 September 2015